Across the Golden Horizon

The Lotus Poetess

ZOE WILLIAMSON

Order this book online at www.trafford.com
or email orders@trafford.com

Most Trafford titles are also available at major online book retailers.

Cover Design by RJ Hughes, Nvision Arts Media.

Print information available on the last page.

ISBN: 978-1-4907-6344-6 (sc)
ISBN: 978-1-4907-6343-9 (e)

Trafford rev. 09/28/2015

Trafford
PUBLISHING®   www.trafford.com

North America & international
toll-free: 1 888 232 4444 (USA & Canada)
fax: 812 355 4082

Contents

GRATITUDE

For my beloved four children, Giselle, Rose, Eli, and Leo.
My angels of reason, and sweetbuds of discovery,and all things beautiful,
of lessons loved and learned, my seedlings of immense hope and courage
Born of heart love and expressions of so much more to know
I am forever grateful on meeting you all again,
spread your wisdom into this world,
let them know you are here.

And for RJ Hughes, my truelove of kuon ganjo,who makes sense to the
unbelievable, my muse without equal, beyond compare
Who taught me that even Buddhas fall in love
And renews hope to me, remaining true to a promise of a thousand
lifetimes, for his belief in me, I am honoured beyond all comparison.

Allow this moment to draw us beyond our own limits
I take us much further still, Across the golden horizon....

Foreword

"How do I describe that which defies the confinement of mere description?

For me, a most perplexing challenge, I aptly concede, and, indeed, must admit to large degree, a task large, near formidable, as to nearly cause torrid lament.

For it is such a task of near impossibility, of daunting providence, as to nearly transgress upon the realm of absurdity and folly, which decries the weakest of foibles which fault me, which fail me, of which I am guilty as a bee's delight in it's gathering of life giving pollens, ... for I am a simple man of limited skill and modest mean, and to be so chosen, to be so honored, delights, yet, humbles me, where afforded this precious task.

For like the industrious bee, how can I describe the full wonder, glories, the essential fortune allowed me by the gracious and magnificent flower - upon whose richest and most precious pollens I treasure and cherish, where I toil and labor to extent in joyous effort to sate both needs and desires - while foremost serving providence and primary destinies of propagated life?

Within, upon, beside and around her, I busily buzz and allow her gold dust fortunes to cover me in her delicious offerings, as I happily serve her essentials.

And though I may be ill equipped to find means of defining her, it is enough, yes, it it is enough, that she is, that she opens her petals to me, that I need her, and that she allows, entrusts, in me her most precious treasures to affirm and celebrate life, and, indeed, that she is a beautiful and rare beauty that exists in sweetest manifestation.

Is it possible to capture the wind? Not truly, although it may be borrowed, may be used to serve many and no ends, may be known intimately, but, alas, it is a fact, it can not and shall not be owned, mastered, or constrained. She will blow, gentle, or will rage fiercely, as is her want and need, surely. For want and purpose, by ingenuity and thrifty design, she may allow in grace, opportunity for mutual unity in service to functions found useful, but she shall never be conquered, never be held back, never denied.

Such it is, in essence and effect, to know such joys as to see her, to love her, to wonder and appreciate her, to amaze at her gifts, to honor her, to be so honored, to know that she is.

Where now I find myself in blissful privilege, yet, near vain attempt, to describe her, to describe and find particular boundaries of definition to honor her gifts, adequately, truly, surely, ... where no boundaries of thought, word or refinement may apply.

Much as a bird trying to describe the air in which it flies, of opportunity and circumstance where evidence speaks of mutual union, or of fish the water in which they swim, of which intimacy is strongly held, evidence plain of the union experienced and observed in full abundance, yet, beyond that, attempts at confining this by mere description must fail. For such definitions which may do true honor simply do not exist anywhere, at least, not within the confines of the simple and limiting vocabulary of mortals.

For me, it is enough that she is, that she exists, that she allows me grace of her gifts, and that I exist in this moment, this time, this life, in which I may love, cherish, that I may adore her, may celebrate her precious rarities of wondrous mystery, ... that I am allowed such rare fortune to know her, to feel her, even if never fully, even though, truly, in my bliss of absolute joys, in my desire to honor her, I may seek to describe that which defies all confinements of description, so that the entirety of the universe may know, at least in part, of her glorious wonders.

She exists, her gifts preciously offered, …. that is enough, it is enough, for she refines every meaning, every purpose sought, fought, understood or not, every cause made thus far, … like a flower glorious and gorgeous in it's own right, yet, not truly served until attended by the dedicated bees that serve to pollinate her, to adorn and share her gifts.

Thus, it is, she is, for me, … this wondrous mystery and cherished gift of nature.
Immaculate and perfected in her essence, in mutual benefit I must love her and rejoice in her glories, and, or me, that is enough. She is enough!"

-- RJ Hughes, Nvision Arts Media.

In the world of the surreal, I believe, there is a place where we all belong. I love as does nature and natural beauty like the throbbing heart beat among us, and when writing, unique and special people come alive to the song of the universe.....

May you receive todays good fortunes with a happy heart, with unfailing determination to go even further...

Always take the risk and believe in such magnificent hope .... Now I fly .... continue forward .

Tomorrow will happen, no doubt, but right now the beauty has already begun...

Sometimes a writer drifts..... in the absence of words creates paintings of the mystic, but everything is inspiration

I am a writer, I must create from what I see, I feel, I sense.................

Perfection upon the everlasting moment of somewhere where impossible seemingly fits yet the moment our dreams become tangible is that time when possible is reachable. When your love is found allow yourself to bathe in the beauty of this love....and begin the journey together......sleep a journey of absolute possibility.

I take us now up higher and further and explore how our spiritual selves examine that and those we cannot understand on a daily basis.

Accepting the line of the horizon is definite and is drawn in curve by nature but is it impossible to cross? An artist can take a brush and paint however he sees the world thereafter as can a musician create notes to accompany the place his inner self searches or a poet defining philosophy with words, yet best illustrated are the perceptions far beyond how we see as fathomable.

Let me take you further still, join me into the horizon....

Zoe Williamson.

Of the Heart of the Beloved

Upon a journey of endless possibilities
I dream the nocturnal
Diamond moon in tranquil silence
Deliver my promise
To the desire of my heart

Allow him echoes of pledges sung
In harmony
With the fortunes of kuon ganjo
And may he meet me
Beyond the golden horizon

Upon our eternal mystical thread
I dance his music
I sleep his dreams
I promised my love for him
Until the everlasting

From the heart of the beloved
Hear murmurs of distant past voices
Sing his name.

You are a prince of a thousand dreams
You are one kiss to my eternal
You are a masterpiece and I gaze on
Upon the everlasting
My love is timeless

you are ageless
Together we are endless
I am sewn into thoughts between us
Golden fortunes
along tapestries of history and future

By my token of lifetimes love
I pledge once more
I remain loyal to my true love's vows
I am yours forever
My love my heart connection

And verity says
whom amongst us all
would not offer gratitude
My prayers share humble givings
I love you another million lifetimes yet

An eternal thread of gold
fastened across the horizon yonder
inflamed by the passion of the sun
Against darkening skies
Overcast in black clouds

Wind and rain relentlessly persist
And may they continue
Because to live inside your love
Is great hope enough
and sensual comfort for me, my prince...

"In my life ... nothing else matters
But that you are by my side
In my life ... nothing could ever be greater
Than the love I have seen in your eyes" (R J Hughes)

And we are found within the heart of the skies
we are those lotus blooms
that have flourished from muddy waters
to reach the impossible
against the indeterminable, the improbable

We are bursting through what was perceived unfathomable
and I meet you across the skies
and here we dance the eternal
Singing the song that defines the universe
I clutch your hand in endless grasp

We fly the nocturnal in ceaseless wonder
I bathe in the freedom as you wash me
your love is golden splendour
And you are my Kuon Ganjo Prince

You were the endless thread of the mystic
I braided carefully
Knowing it would find harmony in your heart
When I discovered you once more
Yet such beauty in you leaves me breathless

Ours is a love of endless lifetimes
Ours is the story of the silver shed starlight betrothed
You are my heartbeat in every lifetime
I recognize you way past all first beginnings
and we shine in diamond radiance

Sweet moon carry my words across silent hushed waters
to the place where my truelove dwells
Deliver serenity and fasten this golden laced thread from my heart to his.

My path is yours into the everlasting sunrise
The horizon beyond the inexplicable
Glistens in hues of golden streams
As our blossoms of lotus wonder unfold against the skies
open as a canvas of pastels

I request on a heart so aroused by this mystical fortune
We fly through our dreams and catch them in our victories
"Wind and rain relentlessly persist
And may they continue
Because to live inside your love
Is great hope enough
and sensual comfort for me, my prince

The Mystical Prince Of Kuon Ganjo

I have loved you
Upon a pledge of a thousand lifetimes
When the time before all beginnings
Has become sunrise gold
At the mists of the first horizon.....

It has always existed without doubt in fervour and faith.

You do not cry out for the misfortunes

What can be replaced
Instead of lifetimes of love lived
Against conforming wishes

Our moments are as precious gems
Sewn together through sentiment
And life experience

These contain the intimate and profound special
Unique to ourselves
And recognised upon each birthing fortune together

Myoho Love

Take opportunity
In exaltation of this crowned possibility
His queen and our
Indeterminably reign

I cannot describe the taste
Of joy
Graciously received
And harvested by the side of hope

Fresh in delivered promise
From the transulence crystal
Of our sister moon in brilliance

And if you exist to love me
Then know heartfelt, your love is graciously received
Nurturing these seeds of hope
With goodness discovered somewhere within...

You are the wild passions
Of rainbows
In colours, not yet known,
chosen against
A backdrop of sunset quiet

In descent behind Eastern horizons
Hues of gold and silvers
Reach past the unreal

Circling the Earth
Aligning the planets
And reigning in majesty at your wonder

Our gentle song
Is heard beyond the simple nightflow
And imprints our cause with splendour
Encased within each star

Waking adrift the moondust songs sung by my lover to the golden chimes of connection,roaming fields of rain coloured roses where the purple grass sways and the breezes contain silver thread impulses of love immortal, cherishing the deep blue sun, inspiring our sensual moon and her arrival. With her I bathe the sweet fortune sent by you upon rivers of white gold and diamonds...I match the longing in your body and desires, your lips pressed upon my wanting skin.

I become the breeze in the mornings, fresh upon your skin, early mists rise and rain soft droplets that refresh you, I am the brilliant sun that shines in radiant awe about you....

Each flower in blossom vibrantly coloured finding new home in this Earth unfolding brand new love, throughout eternity, without beginning or end...as is our outstretched dance across a thousand skies
to rhythmically sway to the pulse of the universe, in time with it's hum...
we are of our own heart

Find me prince of unimaginable fortune reigning in modesty yet to feel
I have to sing you to the universe
Find me and dance the golden splendours of kuon ganjo painted before us
injected through us, into me.....fill me, hold me, dance with me into nightime unknown wonders

there were times I thought I might lose my mind so strong were the urgent sensations soaring inside me,
When I saw the fairies dance by the edge of each sunrise, and the sky was lit in silver, I wanted to dream this with you singing across a thousand moonbeams into

the horizon, I sang once for my princess her theme pierced the moonlight she heard my voice when it was implausible,
and I asked for you into unknown tomorrows, I aligned the planets and positioned the moon, and listened to the gentle sounds, and knew you could hear me too.

I love this place my heart resides now
spread your wings sweet gliding lotus swan
prince to the skies in flight.....

The Lotus Prince

Something wonderful happened along the turn of September
I began a brand new journey
Along the Mystical Path
Filled with great hope
And breathtaking adventures.

My tired feet trod warm stones
Paved in marbled wonder
And felt refreshed, re energized,
When I awoke my dream continued….
Such excitement was tangible
And I held on
Losing breath for seconds at a time
My heart began to beat with another…

If I do not catch myself I am lost inside this wonder
I cannot fathom this happening
Not completely
But there is a grand excitement swelling in the air.

Such manifesting magic
Sprinkling sweet comfort as soft rain over me now
But wonder it is
And onward approaching into the unknown it must be

And prevail it must, this has certainty.

We are a hundred ways of a love that grows
You were there in every man I knew
And of the past what seemed a thousand more lifetimes
I discovered such beauty...

There are times I am thinking of him
And truly moments I am inspired

I cannot let go of him
As if I could ever have wanted and did I want that
To lose the seabreeze waves uncurling at my feet
Standing by the shoreline
Overwhelmed by the ocean's placid heartbeat

Realizing that he was flowing through my veins

My love for him existed along the plains of always
Way before any horizon had formed

We met along side the future past of now
Now and forever across several lifetimes
Further than the most profound unknown
Upon the distant past...

And we meet once more along the shorelines
Of the unbelievable overflowing inspirations
I unfold as a lotus
In the magic you have begun in me
Unfolding before you
In colours not before seen
None I recognize
And am in absolute wonder.....as beautiful and defined

There was a distant hum
And it beckoned us
Following course
I am born of your heart flames

My heart is a flame for you and ignites the sun as it rises each morning lifting
the dawn into the sky and I am the colours that blend rose streaked lilac skies in
radiance at your wonder....these flames burn too fiercely, and cannot die....they have
continued to set fire to the horizon eversince the earth began.....
unknown to me and how many others for its unique passion, dedication and immense
ongoing love.......I swim in the magnificence of your love
there was pleasure of a depth unspoken
my hands clasped tightly in yours for the night was trepid
but not uncertain and if fear existed it was humble
a feeling of that which I had only ever witnessed
in everyone else their passions, their kisses, their loves..
It was of unfathomable depth
with a volume of a thousand arias
this ceaseless wonder continued and still does
It is though I have been painted against a backdrop of such splendour
But you my Kuon Ganjo love
Paint me much deeper
With a verity
And this I find resolution
and I could not help but be gracious your splendour so inviting....

I have loved you through the secrets
of men kissed....
whispers of lovers adrift...
I have loved you past so many experiences lived
Alongside journeys I dared to venture
Greater than the turbulence of the roiling oceans
More distant than the morning clouds embracing the horizon....

I have loved you further than my profoundest dreams
longer than the eternal happiness manifesting throughout me....

along the thread of the mystic
I have loved you next to the gentlest of winds,
against the milder breezes blowing across the softest
spring sunrise...
You were always here.

I have always
I will always...

The Moment of Kuon Ganjo Love

From the moment past the first time and beyond all beginnings.......
he set my soul on fire.....
.and I have given eternal gratitude...
.for in him I am home.
Prince to his own pathways.....
.let us fly the universe in a thousand different colours.....
Wind and rain relentlessly persist
And may they continue
Because to live inside your love
Is great hope enough
and sensual comfort for me, my prince...
Let's make the eternal our everlasting
Let us grasp this journey as a union
Receive this kiss to bond to you, my sensuality
unites with yours
Lets fly the universe together.....

If I rest tonight, will you still me,
Will you allay my fast beating heart,
I find you swimming in my head now
So now an eternal promise reveals itself
The true hearted jewels of a vow of such commitment...
...I become a child against your wisdom

Feel me this moment
Touch me this moment
Do not be afraid
And do not lose me
It is upon this arch of a night unknown
That we came together
And I have known you

Within A Knowing

From infinite past, way beyond all beginnings, he remains constant, my heart flows
across a thousand miles to fasten with his…..

Within him I discover unsurpassable strength
He is the mattress to my tired body
As he can protect my sleep by his gentle watch
My cover against the darkest, coldest night

He breathes heart nectar into each morning
And showers me in golden hopefulness
Brings me fresh meaning to the unimaginable
Makes sense of what I cannot see…..

I love him along a thread of absolute certainty
And further along the Mystic
He is the way in my dreams

….where in ages past,
We first met…

Wait for Me by Sunlit Dawn

Wait for me by the sunlit early dawn
as morning rides over gentle into the musk skies
fresh hope breezes
I am there
always there

I can love within a thousand dreams
past the clear skies
splashed across the horizon
into the unknown, and up near
crystal rain clouds
Dancing along the hues of a silver sunrise

I rest now way past trepid depths
blissful in the calm smooth comfort
of a heart offered

Oh my prince of everlasting fortune so great
I wonder in all things gracious
To present my humblest jewels
residing at their deepest inside me
As gifts confident they will be cherished.

I walk alongside you
A path that widens and stretches out before us
Flora avenues of profound emeralds
and fragrant violet blooms...

Of lotus and rose,
velvet unfolding of blossoms

Upon this wonder
my hand discovers yours
palms rest together
fingers wrapped around each others...
and I echo your voice sweet love of the eternal everlasting

I am heard within your dreams
I am found within precious music
Proffered symphonies
heart music only you can manifest

And much more now than yesterday
and growing in time with life in expansion
This is an unknown wonder
Which I enjoy, drawing sweet comfort
Resounding now an eternal promise

Wait for me by the sunlit early dawn
as morning rides over gentle into the musk skies
fresh hope breezes
I am there
always there

Keeper of My Dreams

He is that moment of beauty
Pure, unadulterated,
In a vast sea of turbulence and insecurity....

Keeper of my dreams
stealer of my thoughts
Intimate soul friend of my fantasies
he has locked into me somehow

Soft words
gentle voices
caresses against velvet skin
a kiss to steal my lips
An embrace....

I want them to see him as my eyes have captured him.....

By ten stretches of the mind and something more
I had no idea of how much magic
Could spill from an overfilled heart
the day the sun eclipsed
...... and I am stolen inside me
A feeling that will not leave
Could I shake you free against idle winds
carrying affections....
Would I wish to.....

"You say I am beautiful
In your eyes, I shine,
I have loved you across the promise of forever..."

There are a million ways to describe the passion of my life
And all of them attributed to this, and to him
who had no name, yet became a thousand men in a breath
Upon morning

He knows me deeper than the oceans
And further than the rolling waves.
He is the kindness found in the sweetened birdsong on a morning's innocence
He is the gentle touch
And paves my way through the mountains undiscovered....

Embedded in my mind
In my eyes...
Against my skin...
I send kisses a thousand years long
And embrace the cool winds I trust
To travel westward
and envelop you
perfumed by the fragrant new journey
along the Mystic....

You sleep in my head
Rest in my bones,
Cling to my skin....
You are the edge of each breath

And this of stuff that had no reasoning....
You brought sense to it all wholly

I am younger than tomorrow
and have aged alongside the mountains,
the trees know my past
and the breeze carries my future.....
...I am no age.

I could not let go of him
As if I ever could have or wanted
And did I want to
And lose the gentle seabreeze waves uncurling at my feet
To know I have loved him
Far beyond being in love
Where it becomes centuries old

This is why I recognise him….
And when I asked him if we could make the night last
Upon the promise of forever
He replied
That it had already begun,
who might have known
these inscriptions from heart to paper
were sent from my heart to his
across eternal horizons

And he is you, without doubt
upon an everlasting beauty that rests inside us now

I rejoice my heart's dwelling
I rejoice in you
I am indeed, home

somewhere inside my heart
that still beats quietly.....
Is where I am found . . . .
From impossibility was born the absolute possible....

I am that woman I believe
        I am beauty inside the inside
        of all that I am....
        ....I am queen to my own life
        and find comfort in the man who loves me

Tiger of the Dance of the Hunted

They cannot tame her
She is the tigress upon the mountain of eternal wishes
Covered by perpetual morning mist
indeterminable, unshakable…
She turns to face the arbitrary tongue….and from deep inside she summons a passion
so full, so powerful, frighteningly loud it deafens the skies………. and she roars.

Rise up against these demons and blossom in a hundred different colours ……..
Across the horizon eternal
Sings the one song that opens the universe

There is no persuasion
When sense rhymes with reason
We can blossom in colours that bear no description

We are the tigers upon a mountain of eternal wishes
From the heart of the nocturnal
New sunlight is born

It is told that it is possible to love and love again, to fall in love and remain so or possibly to render heartbroken, unfulfilled, unrequieted...
We have been assured we can love and be loved and yet to never to have known love, to never have tasted the soft allure, to have breathed in the magic that creates when all else crumbles.......is to have suffered the inability to have received the unique wonder of experiencing the heartbeat of another inside your own.

And yet there is love and to recognise love, to feel and inspire create muses, a passion of magic surging from somewhere deeply invested inside, that it can light up a million skies in magnificent illumination

At the first sighting, precious,unmistakable moments of fragile realizations, beauty incarnate, gracious undertakings of affections known before, from kenzoku spirited souls that have met in distant pasts, parelleled universes......and make home within the heart of another they have longed for, and yearned, whispered softly to know and become part of...

In the magic he began in me, setting flames high inside my very being, we met and I knew he was on this instant a loved one of lifetimes past. From a time way beyond all infinite beginnings.......since Kuon Ganjo, my True Love. A love so impassioned, and so known to me, he awoke memories I finally realized as ours and my soul honours his, my heart beats in rhythm with his, he becomes the song of the universe.....

And to let go once discovered….found and brought home, is a near impossibility. It cannot be done. And yet there are knowings that travel alongside Kuon Ganjo

I cannot let go of him. When I found him on the edge of his first world he filled me with his wonder, he completed my days with an eternal wisdom that perhaps will never be explained, as if he could ever be explained. And if I enjoyed him then often I could not find him but this sensation pulsed in me so deeply profound, such concentrated strength that dripped fervidly its way into my bloodstream stayed, reminding me of former lives where our worlds had once collided, back to a time when we had met before.

I remember our pledge on a thousand lovesongs, the moon in brilliant crystal bore witness to our vows, and I would know you as I know the way of the stars, impassioned feelings unallowed to manifest from infinite pasts way past all beginnings to a moment of space where life was ruled against our hearts, and yet with defiance we dared to love anyhow, further than horizons that permitted us to dream, beginning a story of love unlimited without doubt, a love that persevered and prospered.

We promised in earnest to meet again, and wrote promises in the blood of sufferings and into the breezes of the westward sunsets, as the moon would bear silent silver witness to our vows, on parting the last time I heard the whisperings of the wind carry his sweetness "…if not in this lifetime I will see you again in the next…."

..I stretch out my wings to their fullest span and cover the skies in a fantastical flight of the fearless...... my dreams are vivid, you meet me across the horizon.......time disappears and we lock wings above the mortal world flying higher than we could ever have imagined...

My heart is aflame for you and ignites the sun as it rises each morning lifting the dawn into the sky and I am the colours that blend rose streaked lilac skies in radiance at your wonder....these flames burn too fiercely, and cannot die.......they have continued to set fire to the horizon since the earth began..... unknown to me and how many others for its unique passion, dedication and immense ongoing love.......I swim in the magnificence of your love

Rose of Faith

I am unfolding like a velvet rose,
Crafted carefully from faith

I am in the lotus in bloom,
A thousand layers of delicate petals radiant on a reach
For the ultimate....

Walking in radiant moon filled wonder.
Kissed by a secret no more to be left silent
Amongst princes of thousands that appear on endless quests
He reigns above all
And I accept his gracious embraces.

I bathe in the sweet fortune of his love
This treasured heart nectar poured into me
And I am humbled as he shines warmth
And comes alive in me.
I am love and love that he manifests.

The Breath of the Constellations

Soft billowing winds of the lilac breeze
chance this lifetime
next to the eternal
….may you paint me into the sunset
Resting in tranquil golds
May I remain breathless to your touch,
My body still tremble from the soft breath of your voice….
Will the gods trace my outline
And draw the constellations against your outline
From how my eyes perceive.

Of Kuon Ganjo and Love Recovered….

There is immeasurable pain in heartache however it manifests, and all too soon the agonizing confusion pierces like a needle to the most vulnerable, the most tenderhearted….to suffer is too common an occurrence, and yet ….. the hero does appear.

His adventure is not written, he is born to free the spirit, to leave her untamed.

His tread is gentle, as his words soft, and he has eyes as full as the heart that bleeds…….he has love that swims through his veins, and his is a friendship to the improbable, to the unseen, he embraces the unknown……. He is empathy to the raining songs of heartbreak.

He is a thousand dreams……….

Furthest than those profoundest dreams and deeper than the greatest happiness that we can have yet to be completed, he is the most turbulent of roiling oceans, and has held the threads of the mystic and has loved me next to the gentlest winds and milder breezes of the softest sunrise where he leaves…..when I wake I know only too well he has always been inside me, that he has forever flooded my veins, caressing the rose upon my pillow.

He is unlike any I have ever known

…and with this golden rose I follow my heart on a breath against all limitations, toward to full hearted freedom. I long for that journey and my voyage only yet has just begun.

Where sleep refuses the boundaries of compromise

Is the ecstasy he brings to me uncertain hours lay dangerous

I am my self awake, and stay as so until sleep fetches me eternally.

My courage travels farther than the deepest, and when the pages of the book have inscribed our most, profoundest wishes, will be the moment I will wear his crown, in its golden glory, to sing as truth does of shining jewels. I am becoming now, what I had always known, what I have only just realized....

And the gentle artist lays his brush to rest for now

The story continues against the other world past midnight

Where I wait now in the embrace of the lotus birds whom have protected me, and the promise of something that shone within me becomes eternal, I release all ailments that have prevailed inside me, they fly to oblivion, disappear into nothingness and empty waters........

I rise up against my demons,
Once more,
I blossom in a hundred different colours

Inside all desires that have become you
I am more.
Uncertain lovers have walked paths with me
And I have searched countless cultures over and again
Spoken the tongue of many worlds
And slept beneath the widest skies
Underneath the most beautifully orchestrated constellations....

I have encountered people as old as the mountains
And lived a hundred lifetimes
Alongside oceans of knowledge
So deep inside me now....

Recognizing is not for the fainthearted to share
But for a faith so pure, so strong, alive so much so
A path opens before me and once more I must walk.

You are part of this journey and I am glad we met
I am unlike any you will ever meet again.............
And you are of none I have ever known
I have loved you through countless experiences past
So many others since the secrets
And kisses of men
And how the suitors wooed....
Lovers adrift upon foreign journeys

I have always loved you further than
The most profoundest dreams

Longer than the eternal joy of everything
Because you were always the prince amongst mortal men

Greater than the turbulent, roiling oceans
That carry waves
Pounding shorelines

Along the thread of the mystic
I have loved you next to the gentlest winds
And against the mildest breezes…
That could blow across a horizon of softer sunrises
I have always been inside you
I will always be…..

My Treasure of Soft Passion

I hold onto your words and treasure soft passion
Like the fragility of snowdrops,
The velvet touch of a sensual rose
The softer bloom of fuscias......

Against the voluminous backdrop that has pained us
Your song comes alive .....

Your heart beats at pace with mine,
Against mine, against time.....

The Mystical Thread Part 3

Lacing this mystical thread from the silken sensuality
That has been
Have now emanated
And from one body wrapped closest to another
Tasting moistened skin, salted by sweat,
And tread the treasured path deftly crossed by theirs

This is pleasure
A welcomed fantasy, one that may now reveal
But allowing such fantasy an escapade
Across the borders that edge past sanity
And into the unknown, where dreams are born
Where sleep refuses the boundaries of compromise
Is the ecstasy you brought home
To the lovers of the eternal

Uncertain hours lay dangerous
We are ourselves awake
We are the waking self…
And walk the everlasting path …

Next to myself a thousand voices in arias
Become gentle whispers against the sunshine breeze

I can risk the deep,
My courage travels further than the profound
And to the places we have never been…..
Born of the golden rose
Infused with the walk at sunrise
And the shimmers of rainbows of morning beauty
Grant me this,
Indiscernible
Indestructible as you are
My gift alone, give me this sunrise
The ocean horizon aflame
Scarlet and violet in fusion

Unfolding as a velvet rose
Crafted from careful faith
A thousand layers of delicate petals radiant in reach
Of the sun in magnificence
Revealing the potential journey
That is…
Where the music plays

Shake Out Diamonds

Shake out diamonds
Before my eyes, I hear these whisperings in the wind
I feel your breath, above the voices spun as silk into the satin breezes
They circle the moon, agaze on her silver
And rest against me, soft upon my skin…
…only can I now say, begin your journey to be where you must be
But you paint me across the golden cyclorama
Embracing what glory the sun spills forth…
You have touched every part of me
I remain your passion, I am your heart aflame with desire
You cannot lose me, and I will not be gone.
The sun is on fire, but no match for how my body burns in this instant.

Inside the Gentle

There is a gentle hum of birdsong into the breeze of the next world
And against this backdrop of such medicinal splendour
I cannot resist, I do not want to resist you with me
In such imaginings
And how they happen....
free yourself amidst my feeling of me

Dance to the sensation of my body
On your skin..........each droplet sensual, gentle,
This journey is warm, and this passion ignites me.
You have become censored feelings inside me
And my wholeness is aflame..

I am the love that sheds light upon the infinitesimal
I can afford much love on you
The magic cannot stop because two hearts are not together.

There is a reason to you
And I have found it...

Those satin, silken drops fall onto my head
Across my body,
into my heart,
and these alone take me past what has become possible....
Amidst an unknown world through the everlasting
Impossible.....

The Heart's Journey

With brush poised amidst a fusion of words
A pen bleeding eternal incantations, sweeping across a dancing page
Already brushed by the astute hand
Blending the jewels of romance,
Brilliant, and radiant
Mixing oils against words, watercolours on verses,
Compliment gentle fingers as they rest upon the mystical,
His brushes finish their illusion in pictures, and a magic begins pervading the realm
of dreams, exploring a passion to be shared once until the end.
His heart that beat so fiercely
Could leave one restless against the twilight skyline..

How it initiates such brilliance
as sun descends upon pools of crimson
And fire…by the side of the inflamed horizon
His deft hands, alive with colours
In betrothal to her words
Humbled by her colours

A fusion of words against a canvas
Filled with a pulsating rhythm of passions
untold

It cannot be described what has been discovered
But today he became the passion
that clearly swims throughout every part of the universe.

Within Him I Knew

With a passion and great forward approaching, believing in the unusual and all the
beauty he is, how he has appeared in front of me right now and what will happen
tomorrow, I count blessings and receive him well.
And once where heart break resided becomes a world anew and
I remember it well I love this place now.
Have I been asleep in the waking world
Whilst a silent blend of words and invisible love
Crashed down upon the ocean that carried our lives
Back and forth relentlessly.
What appears impossible against the cool nightime skyline
Is simply the highest mountain as yet to climb..

Refresh the spirit
And leave us to fly.

"I want to touch you
Do I dare,
Could it be..

When the sun has burned past the fixed dawn horizon
The tiger moves swift, undefeated

The path becomes wide
and seedlings of hope have blossomed into huge trees
Vast greenery and beautiful flowers.
There is the soft hum of incantations sung
There is a fragrance too
a sweetened perfume of immense hope,
of love to come and wisdom to be felt.

Such dexterity and grace has the tigress
hungry and eager
Ready, determined...

On Unwrapping Good Fortune

May we continue to unwrap good fortune everyday
A brand new adventure
Filled with hidden promises
Unlocked by our own determinations…

I discovered by my own good fortunes
I could climb as high as the stars
The moon guarded messages of secrets
And love so deep knowing that
If you reached up with me

Beginning to awaken in my field of good fortune
When comfort would not surface
It all made sense
And so did you

Beware the gentle hand that uncurls before you
Mindful of its contents
Wisdom is such a great friend in its silence

Sweet Valentine

To have loved, sweet open humble person,
A sainted spirit hunted down
And slain
For love spilled as blood might
Onto cold stone steps
What loss then…..before his lips ever touched hers….

Felt this by the turn of the evening mists
When greys and misty silvers fuse into indigos and near darkness
As the sun flickers red embers
Past the horizon,
After sinking his body into places forbidden
His icy incarceration
No lament for a splintered heart
Who cries for you Valentine

But he carried an untethered heartbeat
until his moments end
And sincerely Valentine
You did crumble at their words
slain and slaughtered

your innocent blood paints the cold grey steps
How will they recount your tale
Those benighted at their own ill hands

For love tendered and unrequited
For hearts dipped in the blood of the hungry

For love enamoured, and performed in secret
Concealed from the pious
Valentine you are a hundred in saints

They do remember you
And you are read across a thousand sunsets
buried into books of the beloved

you are muse to burn the passions
No longer do you suffer
your story has become many.

They tell me to forget my mind,
my passion my thoughts…
And venture forward
Approach the open and shake off the limits
There is ground past the horizon……………
There is an answer, and unknown as it is, I am part of this………

Jewels from a Mystical Thread

When the sun had burned past the fixed dawn horizon
Was when the unimaginable happened
Where I had lost myself somewhere far from the real music
I heard you play
I thought it was a dream
And your eyes firmly upon me I could not believe...
...when I turned I assumed you would vanish
This was no dream and I was trembling
I knew from that moment I would travel every mystical thread for you
That I loved you for however many lifetimes....
That our pledge remained fervent.

Of Heart Connections and Mystical Wonder

Of heart connections and mystical wonder
Inspire me always
with passion of promises
born of Kuon Ganjo
Bring me my love
At last in flavours known
Across this horizon

because my heart yearns him
my eternal love for him
Alive and dancing
for a thousand lifetimes now
And a thousand more at least

I pledge my heart
To my prince of a million heartbeats
I share my life with
A million possibilities

I am yours
upon eternal sunrise
Of the everlasting
I am breathless
Against the flames
Of each crimson sunset
I love you
For the love you bathe me
Clothed in your affections

I love you
Because I always have

Into the Impossible

Shreds of the universe could collapse
Into splinters
Finding me could
Lace fragments of a new world
Into love forming
Caught upon tides
Surfacing West across your sleeping face

I am on the other side of the silver moon
Call to me
Use those wishes granted to us
Such magic will last way past the flickering horizon
Brightened by the fevered aura that sunk the sun

Flames of a brand new sunrise reach out
Touching me, vulnerable,
You could hear the beating of my heart
And I believe as I believe my love
Tonight, after the hours have taken us

I could possibly live forever on a radiant stretch of violet celeste amidst the dawning
skies...
I am yours on an everlasting promise

I would go anywhere with you
If it just meant sharing it with you…

Let me play for you
and make music happen in your heart...........

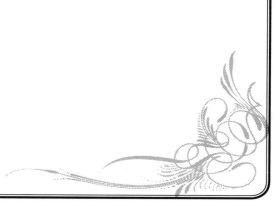

The Snow that Fell

The snow that fell that night
Was not of the ordinary, it was no familiar evening.
Whilst the world slept, unafraid and at peace,
Wrapped up in quilted comfort our dreams began….

With eyes illuminated
And full
When my heart grew as full as the moon bathed in silver

Stars rained softly,
A sprinkling of diamonds glittering
Onto the crisp, whitened ground.
We walked through narrow pathways
And under avenues of arched silver dusted trees
Branches of outstretched arms
Interlacing bony fingers as a crystal silver hooded avenue

Under which we spoke of how many lifetimes past
And laughed
There was an unexplained feeling we were guided toward each other
And those journeys way back
In lifetimes yonder passing now
Travelled foremost and coming alive in front of us
….the gypsy became reborn inside me
And I passionately kissed the breezes
That flew around me in icy gusts
I set her free against tirades of circling clouds
….she is still open on a measure

Of unbelievable dimensions....

I allowed them
They kept me company

We combined the mystical reasonings that led faith
Intuition and romance to blossom amongst the iced pavements
We trod careless, together,
We had loved and that was apparent
Our paths permitting extended meeting once more

Crossing when we nearly fell from despair
My muses awakened so fast and with such ease
I could not pen such inspirations quick enough
I could have withstood the whitest heat
From the flames that burned so high in our twilight

Is it I can still feel you
You became every man I had ever known
you touch me still
...what we discovered against the chilled night
It still burns alive within me

Awake

As I wake
I see myself clearer
More defined…the further I grow

I will share your deepest secrets
I am love for you upon the everlasting
…. I am your dance for eternity……
I am in love with what lies beyond

I am that woman I believe
I am beauty inside the inside
of all that I am....
........I am queen to my own life
and find comfort in my solo perceptions...

I am beauty unsurpassing
I am the dream that recounts
I become everything she holds inside me

He set my heart on fire
And gave opening to new horizons
We watched the sun vanish
Behind a crimson sunset.......

And he strummed me
picking carefully at each heart string
filling the spaces
in sweetness
softness ....

To be adored
A thousand, a million musical notes
spilled in such lovelinessfrom his mouth when he told me he loved me....

A Single Kiss

A single kiss
that lasted a whole lifetime
opened up the entire universe
last night...

Gilded Strength Of Kuon Ganjo

Goodness reigns in and beauty is apparent when it tumbles from us

Have I mentioned we are love and I am that love you feel in every part of me

And what is this love that you pour into me,

From this reckless world of mine, where fear stood second place to me, when I had danced alongside the villains whom crept in stealth outside our windows, before I knew how to run as fast as my dreams would carry me.

I learned tricks that saved my life a million times over, I climbed the barbed wire fences, I fell from razor edged cliffs. But no longer it seems must I dodge bullets, the canons are unloaded, the guns fired out. I do not see them nor look for them anymore, because in mew unfolded wisdom, unlocked by the mystical keys of living, so I learned…..

…..the path has become widened and seedlings of hope have blossomed into huge trees, vast greenery and beautiful flowers. Within the song of the universe there is a fragrance too a sweetened perfume of immense hope, and heartfelt wisdom. Within this year, and every year...

we are exalted and our reign victorious.

You write from a pen crafted from the tides of universal time, and brush away the debris of winds that have blown unceasingly,

We have loved longer than time itself and cannot perish, such challenge fans the flames higher,

My dreams were perfumed by the mystical songs you and I have sung against the most diverse and colourful backdrops. You placed your artists brush once more and painted us into the lilac rose streaked skies this morning and we danced together in a timeliness union, that we learned beyond the first part of all beginnings. It became apparent to me that as the sun rose in golden perfection upon the nightime indigo and the stars swam to her warmth, that she kissed the crystal moon as you embraced me and I gazed at your beauty in gracious wonder, we are found in each other as we have always been. I pledged to you and refresh my vows in honesty, I am yours on an everlasting promise

I have been lined up, strung up, torn to pieces.... And yet by your hand, I am breathless, a child, new learnings, climbing into new beginnings. ... and I am loyal evermore

And so you, your titanium strength covering me, affections richly soaked in wisdom, and such depth allaying the tiniest particles inside me to rest at last. With such valiance I say once more:

You rest upon a masterpiece gilded by half crazed hands concentrated

at easels, an unmitigated work of art, perhaps drawn from beyond every known constellation.

You are a thousand dreams

You are a thousand heartbeats

You are the reasons for this profound mental unravelling that lies unmoved and yet ever growing within the casement of my heart. An invisible link we heard them say;

Not quite like him indeed

And yet ......" in such a short space of time

We met

And the world breathed

We spoke of all things great

I knew I had met you before"

Not quite like him indeed

Not quite like you

Not quite like you ....

The Lotus Princess

I am love and am love that you pour into me
I am ceaseless in the windrush
That carries my love boundless
It matters little the length of time now
You are my magic.....

A True Wanderer

A true nomad does not wander the stretches of the land
It is when the journey furthest reaches the corners of the universe
And the promenade of miles and miles of our minds begins
That is where the tread starts.

The Pledge part 1

I made a promise to unburden my karma
Unburden me from the devils
Reach forward, and pull out what madness was left
….. I will not entertain them again

In Gracious Wonder

Such gratitude for a friendship deepened by love and sweetened by the grace of good fortune that stretches much further than across the ocean, a sea of such passionate fortune, profound in its secretive depth...... our notes of hope, of cherished faith, of committed love are carried across the rhythm of boundless waves, rippling against shorelines, yours tranquil and sanded, warmed by the constant glow of sun, and mine by contrast untouched, wilderness beauty, jagged at cliffpeaks, rocks monumental and unmoved, waves that hurl against white chalked cliff walls, unguided, uncaring.......

The deftness of fingers stroking ocean waves, of beauty overriding the turbulence of untamed waves.....seahorses

pulling in plunder blankets of savage storms forward, and deathly raging of Neptune's wrath.....

To be upturned and over rolled, and thrown to the hungry mouth of each wave in lion's fury, torn to pieces and consumed, grappling for safety amongst the water's merciless dominance....

Nothing is matched to the powerful rawness of nature's beauty, splendour found in droplets tumbled from waves towering, crashing, restless as they pound upon shorelines. Deliverers of messages sent from untamed hearts, to meet somewhere in between in bonded knowing, heartstrings that have braided together lifetimes of great fortunes...... indestructible, and unable to break ever, a braided connection between heart and heart, a unique bonding of mystic fusion, promises, and that one pledge set against the stars where the moon clothed in crystal witnessed our vows. Of the knowing and sweetest surrender to a love bathed in eternal faith balanced at ease upon the music of the universe that calls those whom are betrothed since kuon ganjo and where I swore to love you for eternity.

Upon His Canvas

Who moves from shadows
to night in time to touch me
He knows my tread
And the wilderness inside

When the day quietly closes down
His hands take hold of the sun
And sculptures my world complete with his fingers

They move about me in dance
They create colours never before seen
He mixes pastels in shades of sublime
And brushes past everything inside that feels

He paints me breathless before the sky…
He outlines the moon in crystal
He caresses detail with the strokes of his brush
All around me the world is falling through
I am floating against an ocean calm
The horizon blended into lilac hues

As the sun once more sets fire to the horizon
We chase our dreams
Amidst the evening breeze
…. Lost inside inexplicable bliss
I will forever be a part of your dreams

If it is then that he tells me he exists to love me then it must be, as is written on my heart with his nectar, that I exist to be loved by him.

The Kuon Ganjo Prince And The Lotus Princess
(Upon The Crystal Moon)

A journey that has begun across the horizon
Adventures upon golden paved pathways appear
Threads of somewhere
Happening in timeless union
Along the mystic …..

The crystal moon gazed upon nocturnal oceans
Rippling against midnight
Bathed in quiet starlight

1000 questions posed as she leant against the sails…

"In the stillness and quiet of your mind
The wisest words are often heard"
She had heard him sing

The sky turned a flowing indigo
Streamed with pastels of green, silver
When he mysteriously wove him self into her dreams
Imperceptible by day
And the sonnet of their pledge was relived,
Re dreamed….

He softly spoke;
"I know the universe has everything we need
Await me therefore upon tomorrow innocent and golden
I will appear.....

I will forever be part of your dreams"

And so she asked,
" from the sweetness of angels
You have brought me to my knees

With you such beauty I have not known"

At this moment
The skies unfolded in lilac and soft ocre
As she continued,

"And I dare to seek your presence

You are a prince to the eternal sunrise
And I love you evermore

And we knew this journey would be trepid
Yet never feared the unknown
evenso
How do we leave what we know behind"

He smiled,
" follow me into the heart of the impossible"

As he leaned forward he whispered,

.…it exists……"

And when he clapped his hands and the entire universe lit up.

Upon A Million Lifetimes

My love swims about in your heart...
..I have loved you a million lifetimes
I dream the moon
My love, I do dream the moon

You are the expansive journey once more I cannot wait to venture.

Where the Wild Have Hunted

The tiger determines her surrounds
Alone, concentrated
Follows on and takes her lead

I have arrived at the right place.

Pull up bejewelled, diamond encrusted thrones
Where lions have roared,
And the wolf summons her courage
In exile,
And from where the tigers have growled
And remained unswayed,
unwavered.......

I am undeterred
Shake me otherwise
I will not fall

The tiger's hum is a familiar tune
She jumps into my heart
Listen to the skies,
go beyond.

The sun burst into flames as it descended past the horizon
The ocean a shimmering mirror to its plunging depth
As we vanished beyond its curtain

Across the horizon
And 10 stretches more...
To where the treasures of the heart lies...

Christmas Chill

….thus we found ourselves
Crunching our way through ice and grit
Watching the cold, glistening sun
Our guide
Its silver flames feathered against the brilliance of blue sky
And stretching cloud lines

It was the edge of Autumn
Birthing new Christmas spirit
And invierno chill in natale warmth
Hanging tinsel, falling snow
Reindeer pull a sleigh through air
The magic we drank in sweet childhood
Tumblers full of cinnamon heat
Exists inside still
Because

I found it when
We were not mean to go
That night in years gone by
Thinking we'd lost Christmas Eve
And the years flew by
I still believe
Upon the morning before
We did find Christmas Eve

I was loving us both and happy enough
To continue
We had strength as yet unsurpassed

And we would meet upon the next one.
You would understand finally the rubies that had been offered by me
And still kiss the stars
In radiance that they might
Rain on you this Yuletide
That they might shake illustrious worth
Upon you and you......
And you my love....

There is a winter's delight
And flavours of subtle, gentle love
Always catching my breath
Romantic flavours
Hues of sunset golden and shimmering

You are my golden prince
You are Springtime alive in me
Meet me again next time
....know me...
......wait for me....

My Lotus Prince

And I my Lotus prince
Determine until the final sun kissed horizon

Until the golden sunsets mists away
Until the silver falls to tarnish
Until the heart beat pulses in silence

Inevitable is this joy
Where I have found you
Is now where I stay

My love, my love
my beautiful love
It is you in my heart rides west for,
upon the star laced celeste of blue darkness

I am in flight across lustrous violet hues
left by the sunset
constellations inscribing our love
everlasting
Shine with me into your golden music

You tap into my heartbeat
Your words vibrate each string
Each sound resonant inside my body
You have connected with my heart

What Lies Ahead...

I am what lies in my heart
And seen ahead
Is immense
The ground is shaking
I am rooted in faith
Undeterred by menace

Even tones spread
The canvas is clearing
This vision is golden..........

Untie your wings
Allow yourself to fly

How much fortune arrives from the genuine changing
of one's own karma
astounds me
refreshes me

The crystal moon radiates
And all about us is wise
Yet still do lions sit
Upon jewel encrusted thrones

The diamond moon is fragrant
She broke time
That hung about her like pearls

As timeless as an ancient perception I knew
The precious moon is rose golden
That had breathed life
Into us all
Once

And the song of the universe is well tuned
And lions roar
And senses stimulated

I know this joy.

Whispers

I feel his whispers in my ear
He touches all the places I kept secret…
…he knows me well……

Invisible, quiet, touching silence
He knows me from before

Stretch out with me long past eternity
Your familiarity is all about me
When we spoke of all things great
I knew I had met you before.

Is it I can still feel you
Or can you touch me still
.....something still burns alive within me

..inspired by moon's arrival, she lights up the night in silver, spills stardust upon the dreams caught up by the breezes.......refresh the skies, and dance the eternal...
In love with what lies ahead
in him I find freedom unbeknown to me before
precious breezes
sing to the west of heart connected wonder
written upon the moon
in inks set from his nectars

The stars whisper audibly
Murmurs of the beloved.

Love With You...

Love with you is limitless
You left me against the best side of the universe.

Tonight's sky of pink and cream orange
Outlined in musk violet and velvet greys
Indigo painted cloud streaks
Set in turquoise above a silhouetted skyline...

I am the fresh breeze that rolls from the surf
Of the oceans wide,
In the light winds that carry the sun
You make sense to impossible beginnings

I am perfumed by you
Lavender scented, rose dew fingertips
That touch delicate places
Precious places.

I am the golden lotus
Across a sparkling starspun galaxy
Of unfathomable stars
I unfold about you in a thousand different colours.

I am ageless as are the furthest dreams
I am older than the ancient hills
Younger than the future
I have no age upon yesterday....

A Painted Kiss

My lips rest upon his lips
And my head against his chest
I bury myself into his beating heart
Sinking helplessly into the deepest colours
That he creates tonight.

He shares with me a place I do not want return from
I become the wash he paints on endless canvases
His brushes across the paper
contours
Blending textures,
Manoeuvring an illusion that shines into a work of art
Glistening, magnificient,
Aglow now in dense oils…
She climbed a rainbow, descending a staircase in colour

Undressed before the easel
He has captured everything she is
The wild inside…..
Though he does not know her
His hands explore the savage, untamed stories,
And his skilled fingers craft her every desire
And every need.

Loki and the Prince

My prince I will not surrender in hope of finding you
I will traverse the world twice over and more
I pledged on my return, when I sought refuge in your warmth,
We would unite and these dreams, as yet, remain, unhindered.

So Loki! Why manifest around me
Your disruption simply persuade my actions stronger
And my heart beats harder and me, I am undefeated..

My true prince is not quiet inside me
And you are not everyman I have known
You are though all men I have not understood…

As I wake
I see myself clearer
More defined…the further I grow
And for the sake of everything
Leave me in this piece of mind
I am in love with what lies beyond

Loki leave me!
I am not the genie to your lamp
Let me free now…

He will free me at first glance I am sure
He and only him, can shake out the love
Residing dormant..

He told me when the moon broke in half
He had known me a 1000 lifetimes

I had known that falling in love again
For a 101 different reasons
Could ever be those that you would understand

I saw him in every man beyond comprehension
Time and again he returned in guises
Disappearing in universal shadows
…I search him still.….

Loki leave me! You can entertain me no longer
I am no more the child inside you
No more yours to play

To him, my prince, my sweet beloved,
To be king, to reign in my heart
….the magic does not stop
Just because we are not together.

Our is a love of eternal lifetimes
Ours is a pledge braided in silken vows
Of heartfelt promises
I cannot equal him against another

So Loki!! Vanish
Your mischief is of no new discovery
I rise up against all demons
In a thousand different colours

My prince exists enough in this world to love me
In him I will be found.

The Myoho Princess

You may not win me by taming

I cannot respond so freely
I must be able to look further than the windows of your eyes
I need to be closer to you than either of us believes possible
So that all I can breathe is you...
I must smell you fragrant, perceive every precious piece of you
Your skin against mine
Embracing your cover
With no delusions at all, if, you are whom I can trust
Your princess is not lost to you
Until then
I will live inside you forever

Lower your blade I have no fear.....
I am on the other side of the silver moon
Call to me
Use those wishes granted to us
Such magic will last way past the now flickering horizon
Brightened by the fevered aura that sunk the sun

Indescribable

"I cannot describe what I discovered
But today I became the passion
that clearly swims throughout every part of you...."

.... and if I never feel this again
I will lace together the clouds
Even if the world splintered about me...
....I could feel you, caught upon universal tides that carried me.

Washed up on different shores, tide after tide,
What I have always known, and yet have never known...

I whispered, with you, it is enough

There are places in my heart that I have only recently discovered and they are sweet and profound filled with delicacies and treasured delights. I had believed would only exist in dreams and even then those I dared to imagine, those of others...... how graced I have become, my arms are full, gifts I have never received before...... it is from these recent observed corners with such profusion I send my great feelings of fortune, of love.....of realization, that finally I am found......

You are Each Moment in Me

You are a specific moment in me
And you are all time,
You are time elapsed
There is no name to this calling
No word among the greatest of them all
The cool silver moon of good fortune is rising…..
You are flowing through the universe
Flooding through my veins
You paint my dreams in colours
As yet undiscovered
With each sun as it rises
I can do nothing now
Save surrender finally to the path paved before me.
How radiant is the skyline
Awash with colour
He sees my face…..

In a time filled with history
From a world of ancient, yet renewed vows
She whispered past secrets
Against pain and through his suffering
"You are my prince amongst thousands
You are my dream upon the eternal
There becomes an overflow of magic from your lips."

Theirs were messages carried across the waves of a timeless ocean
Interwoven along crashing waves
Tumbling violently against each other

The rough manes of sea horses galloping at force
To deliver unseeable passion
Before the sun rose at your edge
I could not pen quickly enough the inspiration that surged through me
And when silence finally fell between us
I heard so much
I was almost scared to have known you
To have dared to feel you
I was blessed to have loved you.….

.…how come he still lies beside me.….
is it true I feel him inside me……

The winds are blowing
And the ocean sprays rain like diamonds
He sings in colours unimaginable
And I hear him in everything

Where is he in this world if I cannot see him
Kuon Ganjo narrates our tale
A promise
Closing my eyes I feel him again

I have known him forever
I have loved him past eternity
We have dared the cruelty of time
And have danced the song of the universe
Pledges sewn into constellations
Sung into bursting crescendo,

Unfolding about us in colours of inexplicable beauty
In you there is reason
In you is fragrant offerings of everlasting love.

....I painted my love for you upon the westward moon
As she shimmered in magnificent rose gold
across an eternal indigo sky
Gently lightening to embrace the new morning.

Shimmering moon drop kisses from my lips upon yours
each a promise of lifetimes lived
Together in sensual, entrusted union
I know so well

Because my heart is full
and this I told her
She has listened forever to my silence
and my whispers

She knows my secrets
and from you I keep none,
I bathe in your nectar
I am wrapped in your good fortune

And you are him

I have known him facing countless setting suns
He has provided his arms
to grasp me to his body as my cover.
His warm breath across my skin,
A soft reminder of his protection
and we give thanks to the rose encrusted moon
Our sister messenger
I have found him again.....

How many times have we walked together
through universes parellel
Bejewelled sky now at this nightime

Send my love once more
As it flows sweet honeyed river
flowing from my heart to his.
I tug tighter the braided silks
entwined in gold that fasten our hearts

the moon in shades never seen otherwise
radiant and shimmering
As my whole world awaits him
I send him my love
upon the heartbeat of the fragrant moon
and begin my dance for him and only in his eyes

Will I see my true beauty
Reflecting all he is to me....

where the mountains have been climbed and the essence of the air is such freedom..
Transforming our karmas, defeating devils, and manifesting fortunes......

in him I find elements of freedom unknown to me before.
Waking adrift the moon,
our silver sister on her nocturnal reign upon the skies in their numerous existenc
Songs sung by my lover to the golden chimes of connectionswhere hearts roam and in
fields of coloured roses
the purple grass sways and soft sugar winds billow fragrant silver threads of love

cherishing each other under the deep blue sun
moving to a precious love he fills inside me
Taking me softly against golden breezes to the west
he whispers my name
into the stars that bathe me in his fortune
whispers of the beloved

We are in love with what lies beyond

Among the dreams of the beloved that glisten into the backdrop of tonight
that shines in glory as I find you once more

there flow rivers of white gold and diamonds
where upon the waters they trod carefully together
they danced the magnificent
He tapped his drum and whistled a tune
and the universe responded....

she turned and began to dance
and this would become the eternal dance of the lovers....
where sung the magic that filled her with his fortune

and all this from one lovesong maybe......

precious breeezes paint yourself golden
and arrive to honour the man who shares my love
as I blow my kisses west to him.......

"And so we have no doubt in our hearts, with absolute conviction,
Upon each impassioned heartbeat,
tomorrow will happen we are certain, but right now the beauty has already begun.
Keep moving toward the horizon"

THE END